3 3052 01319 5609

ANIMALS UNDERGROUND
MONGOOSES

EMILY SEBASTIAN

PowerKiDS
press

New York

Published in 2012 by The Rosen Publishing Group, Inc.
29 East 21st Street, New York, NY 10010

First Edition

Editor: Amelie von Zumbusch
Book Design: Julio Gil

Photo Credits: Cover, back cover (armadillo, fox, mongoose), pp. 4–5, 9, 11, 12–13, 14–15, 17, 19, 24 (top left, bottom left, bottom right) Shutterstock.com; back cover (badger) Norbert Rosing/National Geographic/Getty Images; back cover (chipmunk) James Hager/Robert Harding World Imagery/Getty Images; back cover (mole) Geoff du Feu/Stone/Getty Images; pp. 6–7, 24 (top right) Nigel Dennis/Gallo Images/Getty Images; p. 21 Dave Hamman/Gallo Images/Getty Images; p. 23 Frans Lemmens/Iconica/Getty Images.

Library of Congress Cataloging-in-Publication Data

Sebastian, Emily.
 Mongooses / by Emily Sebastian. — 1st ed.
    p. cm. — (Animals underground)
 Includes index.
 ISBN 978-1-4488-4956-7 (library binding) — ISBN 978-1-4488-5062-4 (pbk.) — ISBN 978-1-4488-5063-1 (6-pack)
 1. Mongooses—Juvenile literature. I. Title. II. Series.
 QL737.C235S43 2012
 599.74′2—dc22

                              2010053090

Manufactured in the United States of America

CPSIA Compliance Information: Batch #WS11PK: For Further Information contact Rosen Publishing, New York, New York at 1-800-237-9932

CONTENTS

Mongooses are small but strong.
They are quick, too!

Some mongooses live alone.
Others live in groups, called
bands or packs.

Mongooses live in Africa, Asia, and southern Europe. They make their homes in **burrows**.

There are several kinds of mongooses. The smallest are **dwarf mongooses**.

Yellow mongooses are from southern Africa. They live in deserts and grasslands.

Banded mongoose packs share one burrow. They move burrows every three to five days.

Mongooses are smart hunters. They break open eggs by hitting them against rocks.

Mongooses eat small animals. Bugs, frogs, worms, rats, and birds are among their foods.

Mongooses are brave fighters. They are best known for killing snakes.

Some people raise mongooses. These mongooses hunt snakes and rats for people.

banded mongooses

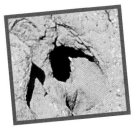

burrow

dwarf mongooses

yellow mongoose

Web Sites

Due to the changing nature of Internet links, PowerKids Press has developed an online list of Web sites related to the subject of this book. This site is updated regularly. Please use this link to access the list: www.powerkidslinks.com/anun/mongoose/